THE SINKING OF THE MIZPAH

and other harrowing tales from fishing with the Swackies

JAMES G WHITELAW

Swackie Ltd

THE SINKING OF THE MIZPAH

CONTENTS

Part 1		3
Introduction		4
1	Who Are The Swackies?	8
2	The Swackie Boats	17
Part 2		30
3	A Typical Week	31
4	The Sinking of the Mizpah	41
5	Eyewitness Account from the Mizpah Deck	53
6	Bags of Dogs	57
7	Broken Wheelhouse Windows	62
8	The Fishermen's Strike	66
9	Injuries	72
10	Summary	76
11	Bonus Chapter - Sail with Jim	78

The sinking of the
The Mizpah
And other harrowing tales from fishing with the
Swackies
By
James G Whitelaw

A special thanks to **John Louie Mitchell**
for background family information
and for proof reading this part of
book before publication.

Also, a special thanks to **Jim Johnston**
for recollecting the day
the Mizpah sank. Also, for his kind
permission to publish his story.

An exceptional thanks to
Jim Bowie, the hero of
the day, without six men
may not have survived.

Part 1

Introduction

I grew up in the fishing community of Macduff, a small village with a population of only four thousand, on the Moray Firth coastline of North-east Scotland, where the vast proportion of boys left school and went to the fishing. That's not to say everyone enjoyed the life; it was a very tough life, away from your family much of the time.

I think it is fair to say that there were three categories of fishermen. The first group loved it and couldn't wait to leave school and get away to sea. While at school, they were, on the whole, never much interested in lessons and would gaze out the window dreaming of the day they would be free. They loved navigation class, and in art class, all they drew were pictures of boats.

At the weekends, early mornings, or evenings, they were to be found hanging around the harbour and often attached themselves to a favourite boat. They would watch for their favourite boat coming in and rush to the harbour to help them land their catch, wash down, clean and repair their gear, and get involved in anything they could.

Occasionally, a boat might have to make a short trip. Perhaps around the bay to have her compass adjusted or to move to a different port. This was an opportunity for these eager lads to get out on the water and the highlight of their year. Many of these guys chose to go to sea every time there was a school holiday from as young as 12 years old.

You were much more likely to belong to this category of boys if your family owned a fishing boat, especially if your father skippered one of the boats.

The second group of boys were ordinary boys who grew up and saw the fishing as an available job when they left school. The fishing employed large numbers of people in those days and paid better money than working ashore. Most of your mates were going to the fishing, and you could see the difference between those who went to the fishing and those who didn't. The young fishermen had big flashy cars and plenty of money to flash around at the weekend, but the guys working ashore were much more on a budget and had an old beat-up motor.

This was the largest group of boys who simply fell into the way of life and liked the benefits. They accepted that perhaps it wasn't the best life, but the compensation made the difference to them, allowing them to establish themselves on life's ladder comfortably. As they grew, they had funds and did not have to stop and consider whether they could afford to get married, start a family, buy a house, go on foreign holidays and a hundred other small things. In general, the compensation made up for the hard life.

The third group of boys, to which I belonged, weren't much interested in going to the fishing but were forced into it by lack of alternatives. It might not be that no other job was available, but that no other decent-paying job was available.

When I left school, I initially worked as a trainee storeman at Borough Briggs Motors in Elgin, where my parents stayed. At the end of every week, I got my pay packet with £14.10 inside, and it was a struggle to make it last until the end of the following week. I liked the job well enough, but when I saw my cousin, Robert, who was around the same age as me, coming home every week with over £100 in his pocket, it was a strong pull in that direction.

However, I was still cautious and decided to take one week's holiday to go to sea on my uncle's boat and see what the job was like. When you went to sea on that basis, nobody woke you in the morning. Instead, you got up when you wakened and helped around the deck as you could. Probably, I didn't get a complete and accurate picture of the job that week, but when, at the end of the week, my uncle gave me a pay packet with £60 in it, my fate was sealed, and I decided to quit my job ashore and go to the fishing.

Of course, when you think about skippers, there are fishermen, and there are good fishermen. The trick was to get a good berth, stick with it, and watch the cash roll in. That did not work well for me in the first year, as a good berth was not easy to get if you had no experience.

I landed the first berth aboard the Remembrance with Dodie Mackie as skipper. The mate was Banffie from Macduff. His proper name was William (Bill) Thompson, I think. Banffie had been a skipper with his own boat before and had quite a lot of local knowledge and was an excellent help to Dodie, a first-time skipper.

I was on the Remembrance for six months and certainly didn't make big money there. Many weeks we did not catch enough to cover our expenses and only got a 'sub', which had to be paid back later when we caught more. But, of more importance, in six months, I didn't learn very much at all and was still not an experienced fisherman who other skippers would be glad to have as a crew member.

After I left the Remembrance, I jumped around from boat to boat for a while, covering for men who were off, but in that position, you get tolerated, not learnt, so I still did not prosper much in learning the job. Then, in late summer 1977, Duthie Geddes was taking three months off from my uncle Robert's boat, the Mizpah, to go and sit his 'mate's ticket', so I got my first break and a three-month guarantee of work.

On the Mizpah, they still looked at me as a temporary position, so they did not push me, which I probably needed. After the three months, I had made good money, even on my 'half share', and learned a little, but I was by no means a proper fisherman.

A few weeks later, my grandfather told me that my uncle John would take on an extra man after the new year and that I could start there on a half-share. This was to be my first real berth, which would make me a real fisherman. The crew were my Uncle John, as skipper, the Mate and driver(engineer), his brother-in-law, Joe Watt, Old Johnny Raffan, Colin Chinchen, Stanley Ross, the skipper's son, James, my cousin and me.

Stanley took it upon himself to take me to task every time I failed to meet the standard, which was quite a lot. Stanley gave me a tough time, and I can honestly say for a while, I hated him. Processing the catch and gutting the fish was a long, laborious job, and speed was everything. I was slow, and Stanley constantly harassed me on this point. Everyone had to work flat out all the time, or the next lot of fish would be up before we had the decks cleared.

After around five months, Stanley was needling me one day. I have to admit, I had probably been daydreaming a little and wasn't going flat out, so he was right to do so. However, I flipped and challenged him to a competition to see who could gut fastest. We both started with an empty basket and as the other crew cheered, we worked flat out to fill our basket.

Some of the other crew started throwing some extra fish into my basket, but I stopped them and was adamant that all the hassle would stop this time. So finally, our baskets came up evenly and were filled simultaneously. I had made my point and proved myself, and from that day on, Stanley never troubled me again, and indeed, we became best of pals.

I have to admit, even as I became proficient as a fisherman, I never really liked the job, and as time passed, I hated it and began to think about how I could escape this life. Many fishermen who weren't committed thought like this and eventually followed other careers.

My uncle John's youngest son started life as a fisherman with his father before returning to school and graduating as an accountant. He carved a very successful career for himself in the financial sector. I have never discussed it with Paul, but I am sure he would say that the hard work and discipline he learned at the fishing was a good learning curve which has helped in many other industries.

That's probably enough of an introduction, so let's take a quick look at who the Swackies were.

CHAPTER 1

Who Are The Swackies?

Swackie was a byname to a family who went by the actual name of Mitchell. In my earlier days, if you mentioned Swackies to anyone connected with the fishing between Aberdeen and Inverness, they knew exactly who you were talking about. More locally, it didn't have to be a fishing connection; everyone knew them. They were famous, although it may be more proper to term them as infamous.

Going back further than I can remember, there were stories which recall fights on the piers between the brothers. They were a fiery bunch, and although they fought among themselves on many occasions, if any outsider were brave enough to stand against them, they would unite as one to face a common enemy.

The Swackies originated in Lossiemouth, and a story handed down tells of a Spanish ship which went aground off Lossie and a survivor, who could speak no English, could only utter the words 'Michel', which we can assume was his name. The locals called him Mitchell, so the line of the Lossie Mitchells began.

I am not sure when they were first called Swackies, but the name is recognized in Lossie too, so it was before they came further down the coast to live. The term Swack means quick and agile, and it is thought that is why the family got the name.

My great-grandfather was born in Lossiemouth, but the family moved to Whitehills when he was young. He married Louisa Lovie, and they had three children.

The eldest child was my grandfather, James George Mitchell, commonly known in Macduff as 'Auld Swackie'. The next child was Mary Bella, who we always simply called 'Aunty'. The third and final child was John Mitchell, known locally as 'Mitchell'.

The Macduff Swackies were the family descended from James George Mitchell, and the Whitehills Swackies descended from 'Mitchell'. I am sure the Whitehills Swackies have plenty of stories, but in this book, I will concentrate on the Macduff branch of the Swackies, as that is where I have an eyewitness account of the stories I will tell you. However, John Louie, son of Mitchell, has books full of records and stories, so I hope this encourages him to collate and publish his memoirs.

First, in passing, let me give you a summary of the Whitehills Swackies. I hope the Whitehills side of the family will forgive me if I get any of their details wrong, but I will try my best to give you a summary. Mitchell married Dinah and had two sons, Eric and John Louie. Mitchell skippered the Beryl, which he later handed down to John Louie.

Eric got his own boat, first the Onward and later the Bon Accord. He later built a new boat, the Bon Ami, and Oliver McKay took over as skipper of the Bon Accord. The two boats fished together, often working on the west coast of Scotland, out of Kinlochbervie. On the last trip before Christmas 1985, tragedy struck with the vessel hitting the rocks on the dangerous entrance to Loch Inchard. The entire crew of six perished, including the skipper, Eric.

The only positive was that Eric's son, Colin, was on the Bon Accord, not with his father on the Bon Ami. Colin, however, had to watch helplessly as the Bon Ami foundered along with his father and five other very good friends. In the next chapter, I cover the vessels owned by the Swackies in more detail.

Before I move on to the Macduff Swackies, let me point out something more interesting. You may have noted that my great-grandmother was called Louisa, and Mitchell's son was called John Louie. My mother, when I come to it, you will discover she was also called Louisa. Why was this name so prevalent in the family?

Louisa Lovie's mother, my great-great-grandmother, was Betsy Gatt from Pennan, and a story has been handed down from this side of the family which answers this question. During the Napoleonic wars, Betsy Gatt's grandfather went to fight in France. When the fighting was finished, he returned to his life as a fisherman in Pennan. He never spoke much about his time in France, which was common in soldiers returning from a bloody war.

One day, sometime later, the men were mending nets on the harbourside when one of the men remarked that a strange woman and a child were coming down the brae. Betsy Gatt's grandfather looked up and said, " That will be my wife, Louisa".

The men were shocked as this was the first anyone knew he had married while in France. However, no one was more shocked than his existing wife in Pennan. He had committed Bigamy.

The French name has endured in the family since that time, but apart from my sister, Mary Louise, I know of no other in the newer generations with the name.

My grandfather James George Mitchell was born on the 21st of August 1909, a date I always remember, as I was born on his fiftieth birthday, hence I was named after him. He married Mary Hay from Sandend (Sanyne) and had five children. My mother, Louisa (commonly called Louise), was the oldest and was followed by John, Shiela, James(Jim) and Robert(Rab).

I remember my old great-grandfather as an older man sitting in an armchair and my great-grandmother as a cheery, white-haired older woman. To us, they were simply 'Didda and Ma' I don't recall Didda working, as he would have been retired when I remember him, but he also was a fisherman.

My memories of my grandfather are much stronger as he only died in 1980 when I was twenty-one years old. He was a real character who thought outside the box. He was a very go-ahead individual who never laid down the batten until the day he died. I was very young when I remember him having a heart attack, and he never went back to the fishing after that. He was pretty high-strung and could not do anything in half measures, so it mattered little whether he worked at sea or ashore; it would have carried the same stress for him.

I think he formulated a plan to set up their own fish-selling business for their own two boats, as they were currently paying another agent 5% of their catch for this service. I remember his first office, a green garden shed on a waste piece of land near the harbour. My mother and Aunt Sheila helped him with the admin parts, as this would not have been his strong point. Later, he moved to an old house on Crook O' Ness street and converted it into an office.

One day my grandmother was sitting in her chair by the window when an oil tanker drew up at her door. She watched with interest, assuming someone had come to top up her heating tank. She got the shock of her life when my grandfather jumped out of the tanker. She scolded him, 'you don't have a licence to drive a tanker'. He replied that when he got his licence, at that time, they did not distinguish between types of vehicles, and they were simply issued a licence to drive any type of vehicle. He used to proudly tell me, 'I can drive anything apart from a Sherman tank'.

Like the fish selling, he figured there were savings to be made by supplying their own fuel. After this, he also bought 'Kinghorn's garage' in Whitehills. I remember Robert and I got the job of pumping out a contaminated underground diesel tank with a hand pump. Later he set up a fish processing business at the Bankhead in Macduff.

In addition to these ventures, many other men owe their first opportunity to become a skipper to his help and assistance, both financially and practically. Quite a few men have told me that, although they did not need financial help, he had made clear to them that it was available if required.

My mother was the oldest in the family, and she went to Glasgow to train as a cook. While she was in Glasgow, she met my father, a motor mechanic in Kirkintilloch. They settled in Kirkintilloch, but after my father served his three years of national service in the RAF, my grandfather persuaded him to come north and go to the fishing, doubling as the driver, a term given to the crew member designated as the engineer.

My father went to the fishing in 1956, when the Golden Bells was new and served aboard the Bells until the Mizpah was built. He joined the Mizpah, but one year later, he decided to leave the fishing and seek a new career in the local health board.

One day while beginning a tow, one of the crew forgot to latch the roller on the stern of the boat. As a result, when the vessel rolled, one of the ropes jumped out, knocking my father, Jim Johnstone and Mikey Clark over the side into the water.

It was a relatively calm day, and the men managed to get back on board quickly enough, which was fortunate for my father, considering he never learned to swim. However, although retrieved safely, I believe my father took a different view of the fishing after that, which eventually led to his decision to change career.

My father went on to have a very successful career in the health service, rising to District Administrator and running ten hospitals around the Elgin area. Meanwhile, after raising us kids, my mother returned to school meals service, serving as head cook in Macduff Transition, Banff Academy and Milnes High in Fochabers, amongst other places.

John was the family's eldest son and took command of his first fishing boat at only twenty-one years of age. John was a massive man at six foot three inches tall, and when having a boat built, he always requested an extra big bunk for himself. Unfortunately, wheelhouses were always a standard six feet in height, so John always had to stoop down at work. So when he ordered the Dioscuri, he ordered a bespoke wheelhouse with an extra six inches of height. This is why the Dioscuri looked different from all other boats built at the time.

John was probably the most successful of the brothers, perhaps because he was the longest at the job. He finally retired and handed the Auriga over to his son James in 1985 after having successfully skippered four vessels over thirty years.

Sheila was the middle child, and where my mother was the one who would do the cooking, Sheila was the one who had to tidy up behind her. Sheila was very organised and needed to be to run the business side of her husband's marine engineering business, which flourished in the seventies and eighties. Sheila married James (Jimmy) Joiner, an engineer at Watties, the forerunner to Macduff shipyards. Jimmy set up on his own in the early seventies, also assured of the trade from the family boats.

The second youngest son was Jim, the thinking member of the family. Jim had to take over the Golden Bells when his father had a heart attack, but he also took over the burgeoning shore-based business when the old man began to falter and needed help. Jim was responsible for expanding, developing and modernising the shore-based business before, in turn, handing the business on to his son Robert.

Last but not least was Robert, often known as Rab. Rab was the wild one and always game for a laugh and fun. Rab lived life to the full but didn't look after himself. Although the youngest, he was the family's first to die, barely turning sixty. Rab was easygoing and, for the most part, simply went along with whatever John and Jim decreed was the best path. Rab always took the path of least resistance. His easy manner belied the idea that he hung on to John's coattails. Rab was an able and astute fisherman. When the fishing changed dramatically, he successfully embraced the twin rig trawling, quickly adapting and largely outfishing similar boats.

To summarize, the Swackies were great fishermen, head and shoulders above most other fishermen, but take them away from the sea and plant them in another business, and they don't outperform as they did at sea. So I think it is fair to say that they were risk takers, which worked well enough at the fishing but doesn't work so well in other businesses. I certainly know this from my own bitter experiences in other businesses.

The only member of the family I can think of who has been very successful outside the fishing is my cousin Paul who has served as financial director and managing director for several medium to large local companies. I can only assume that Paul has more 'Watt' blood running through him than Mitchell blood.

Here is the genealogy of the Macduff Swackies:
Father: James George Mitchell, born in 1909
Mother: Mary Hay, born in 1910
Children:
Louisa Mitchell was born in 1933
married James McGowan Whitelaw, born in 1932 in Kirkintilloch
    Alan James Whitelaw was born in 1956
    Mary Louisa Whitelaw was born in 1957
    James George Whitelaw was born in 1959
    (By the way, that's Me)
    Jenifer Ann Whitelaw was born in 1966
John Hay Mitchell was born in 1934
married Margaret Watt, born in 1934
    James Vivienne Mitchell, born in 1958, died in 2010
    John Hay Mitchell was born in 1961 (Twin)
    Philip Watt Mitchell was born in 1961 (Twin)
    Paul Hay Mitchell was born in 1970
Sheila Mitchell was born in 1936
married James McCallum Joiner(Jimmy Joiner) born 1934
    Beryl Joiner was born in 1964
James (Jim) Mitchell was born in 1938
married Margaret Briggs from Middlesborough
    Robert Mitchell was born in 1959
    Heather Mitchell was born in 1961
    Pamela Mitchell was born in 1967
Robert Mitchell was born in 1944
married Sarah (Sadie) Johnston from Portsoy
    Carol Ann Mitchell was born in 1964
    Ernest James Mitchell was born in 1965
    Gary Mitchell was born in 1971
Second marriage to Anne Stuart, born in 1963
    Further children to this marriage

Apologies if I got any of the above wrong. My memory is still quite good, but definitely past its best.

Well, that is a more comprehensive picture of the Swackies than I originally intended to depict. We are, of course, in this book especially interested in the fishing activities of the Swackies, so in the next chapter, we will look at the long line of boats owned by the Swackies.

CHAPTER 2

The Swackie Boats

The First Beryl – BF357

If we travel into the distant past, I heard the name of a boat being talked about by my mother and my grandfather. The name of that boat was the "Pansy", although I am not sure who owned it. I think it was further back on the Lovie side of the family.

The first boat I could establish coming into ownership of the family was an old small boat they bought from Wick called "Beryl". My great-grandfather and his two sons went to Wick and brought the boat back to Whitehills. This would have been shortly after the conclusion of WW2.

In those early days, we begin to see the emergence of the reckless streak which was necessary to be very successful at the fishing. One day, while fishing in Pennan bay, inside the legal three-mile zone, a local salmon coble approached them to try and find out who they were and report them to the authorities. This would have caused them tremendous problems, so they turned a hose on the small coble, drowning their engine.

The three men recovered their fishing gear and sailed away east until out of sight of the coble and men from Pennan. They then turned offshore until out of sight of land before turning west. When they were far to the west, they turned back to Whitehills, appearing to be coming from the western fishing grounds.

On arriving at Whitehills, the police met them and accused them of fishing in Pennan bay, which they denied, pointing out that everyone had just seen them arrive from the west. This cunning attitude was to remain with the family for a few generations and will show up again in my stories later in the book.

The Second Beryl – BF106

In 1947, after a few prosperous years, the family decided to buy a newer and larger boat. It was also renamed Beryl and was registered BF106 and the boat which set the family on its feet and cemented their reputation as good fishermen. They were doing very well in the second Beryl when a different type of trouble caused a family rift.

My grandfather, James George Mitchell, became a Christian and was disappointed when his younger brother, John, would not follow him down this path. The difference grew to a point where it was decided that the two brothers must split up.

Growing up, there was always a distance between the two sides of the family. There was no fighting, just a cool, distant feeling. I never understood it at the time, but it all stemmed from the point where the two brothers parted company.

The Faithful – BF205

In 1949, James George decided to buy another boat, the Faithful. Unfortunately, tragedy struck in the first few weeks James George owned the boat. The powerful Kelvin 66 engine smashed up, and the boat was inoperable.

Never ones to let the grass grow under their feet, John, in the Beryl, took the Faithful under tow the same day to the Firth of Forth, where she entered the Forth-Clyde Canal and proceeded to the Kelvin works in Glasgow to be re-engined. She was back fishing within two weeks and, for the next seven years, proved to be a profitable investment for James George and his sons, who were now leaving school and entering the family business.

The Golden Bells – BF130

In 1956, James George took delivery of a brand new boat built by John Watt and Sons, Banff. The fifty-six foot Golden Bells was considerably larger and more powerful than the Faithful, with her one hundred and fifty horsepower Gardiner engine.

Twenty-one-year-old John, the son of James George, took over the Faithful, and the Macduff family successfully continued to fish the two boats.

As my grandfather later related, during this period, he achieved a significant dream of having one thousand pounds in his bank. One thousand pounds was an enormous amount of money in those days, which was a considerable achievement. However, he used to tell me that the first thousand was the most difficult.

The Faithful Again – BF267

John continued to fish well in the old Faithful and proved to be a chip off the old block. As he gained experience and spare funds and the boat grew weary, John planned to upgrade his command. John Watt and sons were consulted again, resulting in a replacement boat being built in the Banff yard in 1962.

When she was nearing completion, the yard manager asked John what he would call her, to which John replied, we have been very successful on the last boat, so we will call her "Faithful" again. But, unfortunately, the yard manager did not have the same understanding, and when the nameplates were carved, painted and fitted, they proudly displayed her name as "Faithful Again".

The Third Beryl – BF440

Meanwhile, in Whitehills, John had continued to successfully fish the second Beryl, which was by now a weary twenty-something-year-old vessel. However, as other skippers upgraded their boats, John struggled to keep up with the new catching power and decided he could no longer delay making a further investment.

In 1966, the third Beryl was launched and proved a wise investment for John and his sons, who were now following him into the industry. However, the day she was launched was tinged with sadness, as my great-grandmother, John's mother, passed away on the same day.

The "Bells" changing hands

James George suffered a heart attack around this time, and The Golden Bells, usually referred to as "the Bells", passed to second son Jim to skipper. Jim was assisted by his youngest brother Robert (Rab), who was in his early twenties.

The Mizpah – BF57

The ageing Golden Bells was still performing well when Jim decided it was time to upgrade. The family went to "Tappies" in Buckie (Thompsons) for their new boat this time. I remember this time well, as Robert and I, at nine years old, accompanied my grandfather every Tuesday night to Buckie to inspect the progress.

I always thought the shipyard workers said, "Oh no! Here he comes again; look busy". He must have been a real pain to them, thoroughly inspecting the building of the hull and demanding progress. We enjoyed the outings, though, as we always got Cullen ice cream on the way home.

Before coming home, though, we constantly scoured the harbour area for any Mitchells fish boxes, and it didn't matter how dirty or smelly they were; they went into the boot or even the back seat of the top-of-the-range Ford Granada, much to my granny's annoyance.

I remember the launch of the Mizpah in August 1969, followed by a great feed in the St Andrews Hotel, Buckpool. It was the following year before the Mizpah was ready for sea, but when Jim took command, the Golden Bells once more changed hands, coming under the command of my uncle Robert.

The Mizpah was a much more powerful vessel, a better equipped and finished boat and was equipped with a 320 horsepower Kelvin engine. Her abilities were making brother John think again about his command.

The Dioscuri – BF151

John decided to retain the services of John Watt and sons, who now had a yard in Macduff to build a replacement vessel. People would often inquire where the strange name came from, but John chose it with a few special personal meanings to his family.

Dioscuri was the boat on which the Apostle Paul sailed from Malta to Rome. The Greek name represented the twin Gods, Castor and Pollux, and John having twins in his family, thought this entirely appropriate.

On delivery of the Dioscuri in 1972, George Runcie took over as skipper of the Faithful Again, operating very successfully until he was eventually able to build his new vessel, the Ocean Challenge. After that, the Faithful Again was passed on to Michael Wiseman, even though, by this point, she was old and tired.

It should be noted that the Macduff and Whitehills branch of the family often helped to give budding skippers the opportunity to get a start in the industry by passing on their older vessels to younger eager proteges.

When I attended the launch of the Dioscuri in 1972 at the tender age of twelve, little did I think that I would be one of the crew only seven years later. A great feast followed the launch in Banff's now-defunct Fife Arms Hotel.

My great-grandfather must have been very proud of what his sons and grandsons had achieved. But unfortunately, this was the last launch he attended, and he was very frail at this point, unable to stand for the ceremony.

Mizpah changes hands

In 1970, the Mizpah suffered a tragic accident and a crew member, George Wood, was pulled overboard while shooting the gear. The loss of a man affected Jim quite severely, and he never really recovered from this loss. At the same time, James George was becoming less able to manage the business ashore, and it was decided that Jim would come ashore and look after the shore-based business, and Robert would take over the Mizpah, as the "Bells" was no longer fit for purpose.

Then sinks

Robert took over the Mizpah in 1974 and continued to have great success in her for a further four years. As previously mentioned, I had three months aboard her in late 1977 before becoming a permanent crew member on the Dioscuri.

In November 1978, during one of the worst days I ever witnessed at sea, the Mizpah suffered fatal damage and sank, miraculously, without loss of life. This incident will be covered in detail in a following chapter.

Be Ready – BF337

My uncles knew nothing else apart from the fishing, so had to shrug off the loss and go in search of another boat. A new boat, at least one year away, was not an option, so a search for a second-hand boat was commenced, and the Be Ready was deemed to fit the bill. Only two months after losing the Mizpah, the crew were back at sea on the Be Ready as though nothing had changed.

Robert was to fish the Be Ready for the next 16 years, first as a seine net rig, then as a twin rig prawn trawler as the industry changed. Not only did his two boys end up at sea with their father, but even Carol, his daughter, had a spell as a fisherwoman, much to the crew's consternation.

The Auriga – BF474

Although only eight years old, the Dioscuri had been pushed hard and showed signs of wear and tear. Perhaps that is putting it mildly. When we used to go to the toilet below on a poor night, when the boat gave a big roll, you got a shower with seawater pouring in through the planks. She had served her purpose, and perhaps the sinking of the Mizpah had convinced John that he needed something more substantial.

The Dioscuri was placed on the market towards the end of 1981 and sold quickly to Ireland. John could not see a suitable replacement immediately and hired a boat called the Dauntless to keep us all in a job. She was built as a pelagic boat, so it was very different from what we were used to. The engine was up forward instead of the usual midships, and the aft cabin, where we slept, was uncannily quiet.

We only had the Dauntless for six weeks when John found a suitable boat for sale in the 'South Firth'. The Firth of Forth was always referred to as the 'South Firth', as opposed to our Northern Firth, the Moray Firth.

The Auriga was a strong, able, double-planked vessel with many modern facilities, built in the Eyemouth yard. She had rope reels which were hugely labour-saving, and she even had a proper toilet and shower. We were never used to such luxuries. She also had a mess deck, so you did not have to go below to eat meals. I stayed on the Auriga until I finally left the fishing in 1985.

What's happening in Whitehills, though?

While much was happening in Macduff during the seventies, we have missed the developments in Whitehills. 'Mitchell' continued to be successful with the Beryl and was joined by his two sons, Eric and John Louie. Eric was very ambitious and also, I gather, a little impatient. Eric needed his own vessel and bought the Onward in 1974. The Onward was then sold to MDM fishselling, who eventually put Morrison Ewen in as skipper, and Eric bought the Bon Accord.

Eric fished the Bon Accord successfully and built a replacement, the Bon Ami, in 1979. Like his cousins in Macduff, he retained the older boat, and Oliver McKay became the skipper of the Bon Accord.

The Fourth Beryl – BF411

The Whitehills side of the family looked after their boats better, and they lasted much longer. Even so, at fifteen years old, it was time to upgrade the Beryl to a more modern, efficient vessel. Mitchell finally retired in 1975 and left the Beryl in the hands of John Louie, who had the task of launching and commissioning the fourth Beryl, a modern and capable boat, in 1981.

Mamre Oaks – BF57

My Cousin Robert, not to be confused with Uncle Robert, was a bit like Eric, ambitious and impatient and wanted his own command. He found a hull of a burnt-out Swedish boat in Fraserburgh and bought the boat, and restored it. He set sail after rebuilding the boat in 1983 and emulated the same success his father and uncles enjoyed.

Robert was young, ambitious and determined to be the best. He worked his men hard, but they had good rewards. He pushed everything very hard and perhaps was not the easiest skipper with which to sail.

The Ultimate Tragedy

Fishing is a challenging game, a dangerous job, and I have known many men who lost their lives at sea and boats that simply disappeared and were never heard of again. Tragedy like this stalked the fishing communities, but it was mostly a little removed from you until it struck home to your own family.

When the Mizpah sank, we were fortunate that all the men could get off. Of course, a boat can be replaced, but fathers, sons and husbands are much more precious and priceless.

On the 20th of December 1985, the Bon Ami and the Bon Accord were returning to port at Kinlochbervie. It was the last trip of the year, and everyone was genuinely excited to be going home for Christmas and New Year. Eric was very familiar with these waters, and although it was a tricky entrance, he had navigated it many times.

I do not know what went wrong, but the Bon Ami struck the rocks at the entrance to Loch Inchard, and the weather made it very difficult for any other boats to reach them and offer assistance. There were six crew onboard, and when the vessel broke up, all six lost their lives on the rocky shoreline.

The crew were:

Eric Mitchell (Skipper), 38
John Sim, 26
Matthew McFarlane, 38
David Lovie, 32
Christopher Hunt, 16
Chris McInnes, 38

The Bon Accord, other vessels, and local coastguards watched helplessly as the vessel broke up and sank. One of the observers on the Bon Accord was Skipper Eric's young son, Colin.

The one that got away.
I came ashore to work and set up my own business in 1985, but it didn't work out for me, and I returned to the fishing in 1990 before securing work in the offshore oil industry at the end of 1992. I worked mainly as a relief crew across many twin-rig prawn boats during those two years.

I had become great friends with David West, a successful skipper of his second twin-rig prawn trawler, and he encouraged me to buy my first fishing boat, offering every practical help to get me established.

Along with Alastair Mair, we scraped together a quarter of the required cash, and my uncle and aunt, Jimmy and Sheila Joiner agreed to come up with a further quarter to meet the bank's requirement of half of the price of the boat before they would fund the other half.

Jimmy was keen that we buy the Suilven, which was coming up for sale and which he already knew and maintained. We were so close to purchasing when I was offered my first job offshore.

My life changed direction suddenly in those few weeks, or who knows what would have happened. If we had bought that boat, we would have been committed to a life at sea, and it is unlikely I would ever have gone offshore subsequently.

The Mizpah – BF777

Robert had fished well with the Mamre Oaks and had his eye on a replacement vessel. Having success with rebuilding the Mamre Oaks, once again, Robert opted to buy a hull and have her kitted out to his design. He found a hull built in Sweden and had her towed to Buckie to be fitted out by Herd and McKenzie's yard.

Compared to the small wooden boats we were used to, this steel hull was massive and designed to fish in the wild Atlantic waters all year round. She was a 25m long, 250T stern trawler when completed and worked the deep Atlantic waters west of Shetland, crew changing from Scrabster.

Robert was very successful with her initially, but the Atlantic fishery changed and began to come with many more regulatory restrictions, forcing the Mizpah further afield to find the fish required to cover the hefty expenses this big boat required.

Robert eventually sold the boat in the early 2000s to a new owner in Fraserburgh.

The Fifth Beryl – BF411

In 1995 John Louie decided to upgrade again, retaining the name that had become well-known throughout the local fishing community. The fishing industry was going through many changes at this time, and smaller, older boats were at risk of being left behind. Therefore, if you wanted to continue in the industry and secure the future for your family, upgrades were becoming more critical and regular.

John Louie's son, "Bussy", attended college and obtained his skipper's certification during the next few years, and John Louie encouraged him to learn the skipper's job and take over the boat.

John Louie then formed a partnership with John Watt from Macduff Shipyards to train young skippers, continuing a family tradition of helping budding skippers get a foot on the ladder.

The Sonia Jane – BF31

By this time, I had left the fishing for the offshore industry, and my memory of some of these events is a little hazy, so I hope the reader will forgive me if I get some of the details and dates wrong.

In 1999 Robert and his sons (Ernest and Gary) sold the Be Ready and replaced her with a more modern vessel, the Sonia Jane. When the boys decommissioned this boat in 2008, this represented the last of the Macduff Swackies at the fishing. The torch was then handed to the Whitehills side of the family, who still fish very successfully at the time of printing.

The Sixth Beryl – BF440

As mentioned before, upgrades were becoming more frequent in the industry. Fifty years previously, most boats fished within sight of the land, but over the years, they had to sail further and further to get decent catches.

Into the 2000s, fishing 400 miles west of mainland Scotland at Rockall was a fairly regular occurrence. However, a sturdy vessel was required to operate in these remote, dangerous and wild seas, so John Louie and the boys decided once again to upgrade their command.

The Seventh Beryl – BF440

Although John Louie was no longer going to sea, he was still heavily involved when Colin and 'Bussy' decided it was time again to upgrade in 2019. The bigger boats rarely stop now, so a rolling crew is required. Colin, Eric's son and young John, commonly known to everyone as 'Bussy', skipper the new vessel alternate weeks.

This vessel represents the only fishing boat still operating under a Swackie command. Changed days indeed from the eighties when they operated a total of six vessels between the two families. The industry has changed, and the local cultural position has changed.

Excellent money is to be made in the oil industry with much better conditions and benefits. Locals are more likely to work in the oil industry, meaning that the boats struggle for crew and have had to source crew from as far away as Africa and the Philippines. Many Filipinos work a rota of six months on / 2 months off.

Part 2

CHAPTER 3

A Typical Week

After dinner on a Sunday, I would begin to get a strange taste in the back of my throat. Such was the dread of another week at sea that I could already start to smell and taste the boat, even though I was several miles distant from it.

It didn't take long to grow hate of the job, and the only thing which kept us there was the extremely good money involved, which was not available anywhere else at this point, to unskilled men. It allowed me, at only twenty-one years old, when I got married, to build a brand new bungalow, with one-third of it paid cash. No other job allowed that.

A typical Sunday consisted of Church in the morning followed by a traditional Sunday lunch with all the trimmings. The afternoon would be a subdued affair as setting sail again loomed before me. After Church in the early evening, it was more or less home and then changed into my fishing clothes, which certainly smelt of the boat, despite the strongest washing powder and fabric conditioner.

I would make my way to Macduff harbour slightly before 9:00 pm. The driver was already there with the engine running, as it needed a good while to heat up and settle in. It was dangerous to start an engine and leave the harbour too soon. If you start your car, take off, and breakdown 100 yards along the road, its an inconvenience, but if your boat engine stops 100 yards beyond the pier, then you risk landing on the rocks, which is fatal, so you had to ensure the engine was well settled before leaving the harbour. Once started, the engine would usually have to run continuously until you were tied up alongside three or four days later.

As the cook, I arrived slightly before the rest of the men and started stowing away our food supplies. Everything had to be jammed into the cupboards to stop it from moving around. There was nothing worse than trying to sleep when a loose tin was rolling back and forth every few seconds, clunk, clunk.

When the remainder of the men arrived, they would make the boat ready for sea, including singling up the ropes. When moored in the harbour, you would have out multiple ropes in case one of them chaffed and broke with the boat's movement. Singling up consisted of removing the extra ropes, ready to leave as soon as the skipper appeared.

In those days, Macduff harbour was bustling, and you seldom could get a pier side berth. Instead, you had to berth alongside another boat, often up to six boats off. Every harbour up and down the coast was the same, with fishing boats employing countless men.

The crew would also check that all our gear was tied down, especially if we expected rough weather, which may result in our gear being washed overboard. Another essential check was that the lids to all tanks were secure. Water in your fuel would not end well. There were also a few times when the lid to the freshwater tank was not replaced, and when we filled the kettle to make tea on Monday morning, we discovered that our entire water supply was now salt water. In these circumstances, we had to melt ice for our fresh water. It was not ideal as there was some ammonia additive in the ice, and you started to develop a sore throat after a couple of days.

The gear would also be prepared for the following day; the Dahn attached to our ropes and only needed to be unleashed and thrown overboard when we reached our fishing grounds. The minimum net mesh size was 80mm, which had recently increased from 70mm as a conservation effort to allow smaller fish to escape and breed. As we fished predominantly for smaller fish, that affected our catch considerably.

Every Sunday night, we would remove the 'show' cod-end and put on the smaller one, which was hidden down the foxhole all weekend in case any fishery officers were around. But, of course, that would not be done yet. Before we did that, we would wait until we were out of the harbour, away from prying eyes.

Last to appear on a Sunday night, at the stroke of 9:30 pm, was the skipper and his son James. Although keen when young, at this point, 'Big John' was, by now, no keener than I was. Moreover, the entire job had become a rat race with ever-increasing government involvement and overreaching bureaucracy which took the joy out of the job.

The skipper would head straight for the wheelhouse and switch on all his electronic equipment. Essential was the GPS, and before it existed, the Decca receiver, which told you your approximate position. But, of course, these had to be set up correctly and checked while you knew your exact position.

Once you were out at sea, you depended on these electronic devices for your location. If they were out, then you would be shooting your gear blind and could be caught in obstructions on the seabed which you knew were there.

A considerable part of the skipper's job was keeping his charts up to date. The charts told him what obstructions were on the seabed. If one skipper had a problem with a 'fastener', the name for something on the seabed that snagged your gear and ruined your haul, they would broadcast this throughout the fleet, allowing all skippers to update their charts.

Once all the positioning equipment was set up, next would be the communications equipment. Typically, a fishing boat would carry between four and six radios, covering all frequencies and providing redundancy in the event one should become inoperative. Most boats also had two radars, again to provide redundancy. These were crucial during periods of fog and had to be set up correctly and calibrated.

Incidentally, John was the first skipper in Macduff to fit a radar when they became available, earning him the nickname "Scanner".

Next was a complete check on your instrumentation. The skipper had to know that his engine was running well and settled in, with no alarms showing. Once completed, the skipper would switch on all his navigation lights and instruct the crew to cast off. Navigating out of the harbour can be difficult if there are many boats, and great care was required to clear the harbour into the open sea.

As you sailed down the harbour channel, the crew would look back, watch the land recede, and resign themselves to another few days of gruelling work and precious little sleep. The following eight hours, sailing to the fishing grounds may be the last decent sleep they would have until they returned home.

Before leaving home, the skipper would have spent most of his Sunday on the telephone, talking to other skippers, exchanging news and views and deciding where to head to get the best fishing this week. But, of course, part of that reasoning was determining which skipper was telling you the truth, guessing what they were not telling you and such other considerations.

If a skipper knew there was good fishing in a particular spot, they would not want other boats there, as the fish in that location was finite. Therefore, you wanted to fill your boat before other skippers figured out there was good fishing in that area.

On leaving the harbour, the skipper knew where he was going and would set a course and work out the distance and time to the location. He would then 'set the watch', with the time divided between the crew in equal proportions. Finally, he would keep the last period for himself, which allowed him to talk to other skippers on the radio, get new information and fine-tune his plan for the week.

There was always a discussion on Sunday night, "Who had the first watch on the way in?" The watch was operated on a rota so that no one pulled the bad watch every time. No one liked the second watch or the last one. If you had the second watch, it was barely worth going to bed as you would be called out again in around one hour. If you had the last watch, you called the skipper for the last hour, and it was hardly worth returning to bed.

When satisfied, the skipper would pick an exact spot to commence fishing and call the crew out around ten minutes before reaching the location. No time was to be wasted, and as soon as we reached the location, the skipper would give the signal to throw the Dhan overboard.

We operated the 'siene net' method of fishing. This entailed shooting your ropes in a triangle formation, with the net in the middle. Each side of the ropes was 12 coils long, with a coil being 100 fathoms or 600 feet. Your ropes' total length was 14,400 feet or two and three-quarter miles. Seine net ropes were stiff fibre and laced with lead to give them the weight required to keep them on the bottom. The net would have two wings with an entrance in the middle leading to the 'bag', then 'cod end'. The wings were much bigger mesh and acted as a guide to the fish to drive them towards the entrance. Once the fish entered the bag, the mesh got progressively smaller until the fish were trapped entirely with no opportunity to escape.

Once the Dhan was thrown overboard with our rope secured, the skipper would proceed at full speed, in a straight line for eight coils, before making a 120-degree turn to the left, or the port side, if you know your nautical terms. A further four coils would take you to the end of the first side of the ropes, and we would slow down to shoot the net, a more critical time. Once the net was in the water, the skipper increased speed again and ran another four coils before making another 120-degree turn. As the last of the ropes ran overside, you should be coming back towards your Dhan. The last side of the rope was already connected to the winch, so now we would retrieve our Dhan and connect the first side of the ropes to the winch.

Once connected to the winch, we would commence winding in the ropes slowly while the boat towed the entire rig through the water slowly. As we towed, the ropes, initially forming a 120-degree angle, would slowly close over the next hour. Once the ropes were together, we would switch the winch to fast gear and retrieve the net as fast as possible. Everything was always done at top speed, as more hauls meant more fish and money.

When all the ropes were retrieved, we would transfer the 'sweeps' (wire ropes attached to both the top and bottom of the net) to the hydraulic power block. We would then haul the sweeps, then the net aboard until we came to the cod end where the fish were. The cod-end was then pulled around the side of the boat and hoisted aboard. Once inboard, the rope securing the cod end was released, letting the fish drop into the designated area of the boat.

Other boats watched and listened carefully to how long it took you to haul your net. After getting the fish onboard, the skipper reported his catch to the fleet. Skippers, however, were notable liars and would under-report so that you would not come and crowd the area where the good fishing was. Other skippers would carefully note how long you took to haul your net, indicating how good a haul was. They figured they could not trust you to tell the truth.

As soon as the last fish was aboard, bearing in mind that it may need a number of lifts if you had a good haul, the skipper was concerned with getting the boat to the next location as soon as possible. While he was doing this, the crew were getting the gear ready again. The rope man was forward, tying on the Dhan, ready to shoot. At times he barely got time to do this before it was time to throw it overboard again. The entire haul took around two hours to complete.

Another two or three men were getting the net ready, which would take a little longer. This was not a problem, however, as there were 12 coils to run before the net, leaving them plenty of time to get the net ready for shooting. Of course, this is assuming the net is not damaged. If the net was damaged, then it had to be repaired. If it was severely damaged, then it had to be pulled aside and the spare net run. The net would then be repaired during the next haul, perhaps a few hauls or even overnight. Only on severe damage, we had to wait and take the net onto the pier and spread it out at the end of the week.

When a net got worn, it was replaced with a new net and moved to the spare net box. The spare net was stowed on the wheelhouse roof as a final backup. The previous backup would be sent to the skip.

When everything was ready and we had reached the following shooting location, the entire process would start all over again, and this would be repeated all day, as long as there was daylight. This method of fishing generally only worked in daylight, so we would stop for the night and set the watch again.

This was great in the winter, as you could only get four or five hauls in during daylight. Although we always caught more per haul and worked late into the night clearing the fish, we would still get a decent sleep. However, the summer was the time we hated as we managed to push in eleven hauls a day, allowing only three hours of sleep each night. Even during those three hours, three men had to take an hour's watch each. Pity the poor guy who had the middle watch. He got only one hour in bed, called for a watch and then another hour in bed.

As the cook, during the first haul, I would prepare breakfast. Once breakfast was complete, I would prepare the dinner for later in the day, as often there was never time to do that later in the day. Apart from breakfast and dinner, we would have tea and biscuits every second haul to keep the men going through the day. In the winter, we had dinner when the day was finished, but on the long summer days, we would have dinner instead of tea, one of the hauls.

The process would start all over again early the following day, still tired. Sometimes, in the summer, after a few days, we would be so tired that as we gutted the fish, the tedious process would lull us into sleep. However, we would keep gutting fish, our bodies going through the process, even though we were fast asleep. Eventually, someone would notice and give you a shout to wake up.

We fished until the boat was full. We fished for bulk rather than quality, so we needed a full boat for a decent wage. If we had good fishing, sometimes we got home on Wednesday morning, but usually, it was Thursday morning. From spring through summer, fish were always scarce and often during this period, we often had to fish an extra day, getting home on Friday morning.

We only carried food for three days, so if we had an extra day, as the cook, I would select seven of the choicest haddocks from one of our hauls, fillet them, and they were cooked fresh from the sea. A fresh haddock like this is the one thing I do miss from my days at the fishing.

When we got back into port, everyone helped land the fish and stock up with new boxes and ice, ready for the next week. Then we all turned to our individual jobs. I had to clean the cabin, galley and mess deck. The driver had to complete maintenance and repairs on his equipment while the rest of the crew would check and repair the net and ropes.

By lunchtime, we were ready for home and would usually collapse into bed for a good few hours after a shower. The weekend was before us, and we could enjoy our efforts in whichever way we chose. All too soon, though, it was back to Sunday, and it all began again.

Of course, this was a typical week. All manner of things could turn up to upset your pattern. These included breakdowns, injuries, the need to help another boat with problems, but above all, the weather, which determined your movements and ability to fish.

The Swackies were renowned for fishing in all types of weather, and often we would be the only two boats on the sea when every other boat was tied up in port. At these times, fish on the market were scarce, and you got excellent prices, giving us some of our biggest weeks ever.

We were classed as 'share fishermen'. The total catch was sold, and the expenses were paid, including fuel, gear, food, commission, insurance, and many other items. What was left was divided equally between the boat owners and the crew. Each crew member got an equal share of the crew's allocation unless you were a young lad on a half-share.

The Swackies were always very fair with their 'square-ups', the term given to the division of the total proceeds of your catch. However, not all skippers were so fair, and many skipper's families bought their food or filled their central heating tank at the boat's expense.

This theft of money from the crew became more widespread as the years progressed and grew to proportions which could only be described as fraud. However, this general attitude of fraud and misappropriation of funds was growing in every other industry, so it should not be surprising that boat owners jumped on the bandwagon.

CHAPTER 4

The Sinking of the Mizpah

There were very few Sunday nights when we did not set sail. The Swackies had a reputation for going out when every other boat remained tied up in the harbour. Often they were termed as 'The mad Swacks'. There were, however, some nights when things were in the balance, and Sunday the 12th of November was one of those nights.

I remember the night well, even though it is now over forty-four years in the past. We were moored at the jetty, just behind the fish market at Macduff, closest to the pier, and the Mizpah was on our off-side. All other boats in the harbour were in complete darkness. Every other skipper had already cancelled sailing.

It was one of those nights when even a wind off the land was strong enough to be singing through the rigging, and no one ventured out unless they absolutely had to. Our crew absolutely had to, as the skipper had not called to cancel, and it was, therefore, our duty to turn up.

We all went through our usual routines, although, in the back of our minds, we figured there was a better than even chance we would be going home again, even though we were sailing with the Swackies. We had all seen this before and knew the routine. The two skippers would collude and talk for a while, rubbing their hands and scratching their heads, before agreeing to hold off until they got the 'Midnight 33 forecast'.

The meteorological office issued four shipping forecasts per day, and as fishermen, we listened to every one of them by habit, even in the summertime when the weather was good. If the skipper was in bed, the watch had to listen and write down a summary for the skipper to look at when he got up.

The four forecasts were broadcast on long wave frequency 200kHz. Younger readers may have to google this to see what it means. They were broadcast at exact times. There were a few rousing patriotic tunes (Rule Britannia and such) starting at 05:45 before the first one was broadcast at exactly 05:50 each morning. The second was broadcast after the Archers at exactly 13:55 and the third at 17:55.

We were waiting for the final one of the day, which, although compiled before midnight, was not broadcast until 00:33 the following morning. It was a very familiar sequence to us, with programs for the day finishing at half past midnight; we would then hear the radio presenter say, "To take you up to the shipping forecast, here is 'Sailing by' by Ronald Binge" Sailing by was quite a pleasant tune, one which I can still hear running through my head until this day.

I have been away from fishing for a long time now, so I have absolutely no idea if this routine still continues. In the modern internet age, weather is available on demand at any time of day. Once 'Sailing By' was finished, we would hear more familiar words, "It is now Midnight thirty-three and time for the shipping forecast, issued by the Meteorological Office at twenty-three thirty on Sunday the twelfth of November one thousand, nine hundred and seventy-eight. There are warnings of gales in Viking, Forties, Cromarty, Forth, Tyne, Dogger...........Malin, Tiree, Hebrides, Fair Isle, Faroes and South-East Iceland"

Then the detailed forecast would commence, and we would pay particular attention to Cromarty and Fair Isle as these were our areas of operation. Cromarty would often be less severe as it was a more sheltered area. Fair Isle covered the area around the northern isles and was, therefore, much more exposed. I cannot remember the forecast that evening, but it would have run something like the following. "Fair Isle. South-west severe gale nine to storm force ten, occasionally hurricane force eleven or twelve for a time".

Of course, the shipping forecast only indicated what would happen over the next twenty-four hours. The skipper would already have watched the 'Farmers weekly forecast' shown on BBC just before 1:00 pm every Sunday. He would not have been interested in the part where the forecaster told the farmers how much rain he would get, but instead would have studied closely what the isobars were showing for the week. This week's forecast had shown an enormous low approaching from the Atlantic with very closely packed isobars, indicating extreme winds.

The forecast was not good, and the general feeling was that we should go home. Rab, however, felt that forecasters were unreliable and had got it wrong too much lately. Coincidently, he had been interviewed live on TV only a couple of weeks previously, complaining that the weather forecasters were overestimating the weather. Michael Fish, a prominent BBC forecaster, was to throw this back in Rab's face only the following week after the Mizpah sank.

There was much debate for another 30 minutes until Rab got fed up and declared that he was going to sea. It was a case of 'where one goes, goes all', so we followed him out of the harbour that blustery Monday morning, heading for the 'Jungle', our favourite fishing grounds. We would return on Wednesday, but the Mizpah was never to see Macduff harbour again.

Steaming off to the grounds was easy as we ran before the wind and sea. The boat would still take some funny lurches, but on the whole, she surfed along on top of and before the waves. Only when the wave finally managed to get past us would the boat fall into a trough and wallow for a few seconds before the next wave picked us up, and we continued to surf on the crest.

We reached the fishing grounds, and it seemed like Rab had been correct. The forecasters had overestimated the force of the wind, and although quite rough, we were still able to work as usual, taking things a little slowly. We only managed five hauls that day as we were taking things easy, but also, we had good fishing, which takes each haul a little longer.

It was almost midnight before we finished processing the fish and had eaten dinner. The skipper set the watch for Six O'clock in the morning, reminding the watch to 'take the cast' at Midnight thirty-three. When we got up in the morning, it was still completely dark, but we could feel the weather had deteriorated throughout the night. The wind was howling through the rigging, and there was some debate over the VHF whether we should shoot or whether we should 'dodge' and wait.

When the weather was too bad for working, we would point the boat into the weather with only enough power to keep her head to the wind and wait until the weather subsided. But, again, Rab wasn't keen on dodging. He reasoned that we had had excellent fishing the previous day, and if we could only get in a few more hauls, then we could set sail for home that evening with an outstanding catch, which would inevitably fetch great prices when there were very few boats at sea.

Once again, Rab decided for both skippers, and we started shooting our gear very slowly and cautiously. Time was never to be wasted at this job, so it was always timed to shoot our gear and be started towing before daylight started to arrive. For some strange reason, the best hauls of the day were usually what we termed 'the making of daylight' and 'the darkening'.

The problem was that the weather and seas were often subdued in darkness and increased at daylight. This was not always the case, but it certainly was on Tuesday 14th of November, 1978, when the Mizpah had less than twenty-four hours to remain afloat. During the next hour, while we towed our gear and closed the net, the wind strengthened into the worst day I had ever seen at sea.

If you consider that I was part of a crew regarded throughout the fishing industry as madmen who went to sea in all types of weather, then perhaps you can begin to understand how bad the weather was that day. The wind was so strong that it was whipping the tips of the waves off in a horizontal spray which completely blinded us looking into the wind.

While we were towing, we had been, while not exactly into the wind, at least sheltered in part from its full force on the aft deck. Once the ropes were all in, we would tow the net to the surface, upwind, but not directly upwind, in case we drifted down on top of the net when we started to haul through the power block, when the propellor had to be shut off.

When the skipper finished towing the net up, it was a mad rush to get it into the power block before it started to go down again, and the weather started to push the boat downwind from the net. For the first part of the sweeps, we were drifting down past the net, so it was very easy, but then as we drifted past and were hanging with the net like a sea anchor, things became very difficult.

We had a very powerful hydraulic power block, but even with this power-assisted machine, we often pulled in ten feet only to watch nine feet being yanked back out again. So we had to be very careful where we stood and where we put our hands and fingers. If we were to get caught up in the net, we could be yanked out with it and suffer severe injuries or even fatal consequences.

Never were seven men so glad to see the net retrieved and the fish aboard so the skipper could point the vessel into the face of these hurricane-force winds. There was no more debate now. It was self-evident that to continue fishing was not an option. The only consideration now was what to do for the best. Do we dodge or head for home?

It was academic, as heading the boat into the wind was also the direction of home, so the only thing to decide was how much power to put on. Do we dodge at minimum power or give her a little more power to keep us moving ahead? Dodging was okay if it was for a short time, intending to recommence fishing, but with strong winds, as we had now, it was doubtful we could start fishing again that day or even the next day.

Dodging kept your head to the wind, but in reality, you could be going backwards, which with wind from the southwest, you would be going further away from home, more into the open sea with possibly stronger winds and higher seas. So we had no option but to put more power on the engine and start to edge in the direction of home and 'smaller waters'.

We were under no illusion that this would be an easy day. I can't speak for any of the other crew, but I had never seen a day like this in my few short years at sea and have never seen one since, either on a fishing boat or an oil rig.

We dodged along with every crew member squeezed into the small wheelhouse, just watching the seas coming at us. But, unfortunately, you could only see as far as the next wave crest as the water was streaming off the top, completely obscuring our vision. Then for a brief moment, we would be carried up to the top of the crest where we had a slightly more transparent and more extended vision, but one which you did not want to see as all around us were giant angry waves, crashing onto anything which got in their way.

The Mizpah was one-quarter of a mile on our starboard side, but most of the time, we could not see her. When we were down at the bottom of a trough, and the Mizpah was in the same trough, it was like looking down a long, long tunnel at a distant ship, and then she was gone again. I have never experienced that vision again at any point in my long career at sea.

Again, I can only speak for myself. I had no fear. The Dioscuri was a decent boat in which we had seen some pretty horrendous weather, even though, perhaps not as bad as this. It never occurred to me that perhaps we might be in danger. Of course, I was only nineteen years old, so maybe I was simply young and naïve.

It was 1:00 pm on Tuesday, 13th November, and although we did not yet know, the Mizpah had barely twelve hours left afloat. The VHF crackled, and Rab told us they were taking water, but this was not unduly concerning.

On the Dioscuri, we had a pump which ran almost continuously in bad weather, as the planking was not perfectly waterproof. If the pump had problems, we had a backup pump generally used for fish washing and could be rerouted to pump out the bilges.

We also had an auxiliary engine with a powerful pump that could pump out the bilges in an emergency. Often, things happened on a boat, resulting in an excess take on of water, especially in poor weather and high seas.

On the Mizpah, the driver would go below to put on more pumps, while some of the other crew would go forward and sound the spaces to see if there was a problem. No case for concern at this point. However, only fifteen minutes later, Rab contacted us and told us that the crew had reported five feet of water in the main hold.

This was very concerning as the main hold was only around ten feet high, so it was already half filled with water and had begun seeping into the engine room. The air intake for the engine was around six feet high in the engine room. If the water reached this height, the water would flood the engine, rendering the boat powerless. No power meant no ability to pump out the intake of water. Once the engine stopped, it was basically all over.

The Mizpah crew continued to investigate to see if pump intakes were blocked or if there were any other ways of pumping out the excess water. However, by two-thirty, it was apparent that they could not stem the flood of water and the coastguards were alerted, and a search and rescue helicopter was scrambled.

The crew of the Mizpah were now resigned that the boat was sinking beneath them and looked to the helicopter heading in their direction as their salvation. By this time, other vessels on the sea had also been alerted through the standard emergency channels, and some were being managed by the coastguards, standing by to offer assistance if required.

Around three-thirty in the afternoon, the helicopter arrived on location and commenced rescue operations. Before the helicopter can commence rescue operations, the first step is to establish a connection with the vessel. Once a connection is established, the helicopter can hover offset to the vessel and conduct operations without the risk of coming into contact with the vessel's mast and rigging, which could be fatal.

The helicopter passes down a thin line to the vessel with a weak link in case it gets snagged. This operation is the most dangerous as it must be done with the helicopter directly overhead the vessel. This is particularly a problem in small fishing vessels, as they have high multiple masts and superstructures spread over the entire deck. To get the line to the deck, the helicopter crew must get the messenger line down without snagging anything on the way, which is very difficult when a boat is bobbing around wildly in a hurricane force twelve.

The crew tried three times to establish a line but were unsuccessful on all three occasions. The pilot was to tell us later that while he hovered overhead, sometimes there was a seventy-foot gap, and at other times the masts almost came into contact with the helicopter. Eventually, the helicopter, having limited fuel aboard, had to give the crew of the Mizpah a distressing choice.

It was clear that the helicopter would not be able to lift the crew off the boat, so to conclude the rescue, the crew would be required to take to a liferaft where the helicopter crew knew they could reach them without obstructions in the way. I can fully understand the reluctance of the crew to board a flimsy liferaft in these mountainous seas, but what was the alternative?

While the crew considered this, the helicopter became critically low on fuel. So it departed for base to refuel, with the possibility of returning, although it would certainly be dark by the time they could return. Meanwhile, the coastguards, working in the background, had located a larger vessel in the vicinity.

Aberdeen-based Millwood had concluded a three-week trip in Icelandic waters and was heading home to land their catch on Wednesday morning. However, the coastguards diverted the vessel towards our location and were now formulating a plan for the Millwood to carry out a rescue operation.

We could not go alongside the Mizpah as wooden boats would be in danger if they came into heavy contact with each other. It could well end up with two vessels being lost instead of one, two crews being lost instead of one. A larger steel vessel provided a more viable option, which, while it could still damage the Mizpah, posed little risk to the Millwood being a far sturdier build. The Mizpah was already doomed, so the only concern was staying afloat long enough to get the crew off.

The Millwood arrived on location shortly before 6:00 pm and sailed around to size up the situation. Her master, Jim Bowie, consulted with Rab and John about how best to proceed. It was decided that we would go upwind and stand by to spread some oil onto the sea. Have you ever heard the term 'spreading oil on troubled waters'? There is a reason for this saying. In difficult seas, a thin layer of oil prevents the waves from breaking and briefly calms the sea.

Calming the seas was to be our contribution and hopefully enough to allow the Millwood long enough to go alongside the Mizpah and get the men off. So, while we moved some of our barrels of engine oil from our engine room up to the deck, the Millwood, aware that the Mizpah could sink at any moment, started to get into position on the windward side of the Mizpah. This was the safe side as they would not want the Mizpah drifting down on top of them.

We emptied four five-gallon drums of thick engine oil overboard. When the oil spread down to the area of the Mizpah, the Millwood darted in to come alongside the forward end of the Mizpah, where the deck was higher, and the Millwood would not be towering so high above the Mizpah. It was all over in seconds, and the Millwood pulled out again to avoid damage.

Then the news was handed down to us that only four of the crew had managed to get off, and there was still a further two onboard the stricken vessel. So the Millwood would have it all to do again to attempt to rescue the remaining crew members. Fortunately, Skipper Bowie was calm and level-headed and wasted no time in moving back alongside and almost before we knew it, the entire Mizpah crew had been plucked to safety.

As the Millwood continued her journey towards Aberdeen, the coastguards stood down all parties on standby as the crisis was over. However, as we watched the Millwood disappear to the south, our skipper, John, had other concerns on his mind. As far as the coastguards were concerned, the operation was complete, but John had a financial stake in the Mizpah and had begun to assess what that meant for him.

It is amazing! You think you are the only two boats on the sea, but other vessels appear out of nowhere when something happens. Firstly, a salvage tug, the 'Yorkshireman', appeared on the scene, and John was starting to think about what kind of claim would arise if the tug were able to salvage the Mizpah.

Around 6 pm, when the crew were rescued, the wind was howling, but two hours later, the wind had died completely down to zero. We must have been in the eye of the storm, and the sea had dramatically subsided. John thought this was his opportunity to do something and hatched a plan to take the Mizpah under tow by the stern and tow her to Wick, which was only some thirty miles distant.

Two hours after the crew were plucked to safety, we were bumping alongside the Mizpah, stern to stern, with John issuing instructions for his son James to jump aboard and secure a rope. James refused to board a sinking vessel, and we pulled off again. John had planned to take her in tow and have a man standing by with an axe to cut the rope if she suddenly sank. I think it was a scary idea and probably was well, we did not carry out this plan.

We stood by the Mizpah, unsure about what to do next, when another boat appeared on the scene. You may remember, at the beginning of the book, I outlined the origins of the Swackies and told you about my grandfather, James George and his brother John. I didn't say much about his sister as she didn't figure in the fishing narrative. Not only was she a woman, but also, her family were all girls.

However, Mary Bella's oldest daughter married a Portsoy man called George Sutherland, known locally by the bye-name 'Hatties'. This same George Sutherland appeared in his boat, the appropriate named 'Sans Peur', a French name with the literal translation, Without Fear.

Four boats floated around, and nobody was sure what to do. So we hung around and discussed a few ideas until past midnight, and then John thought it best we get some sleep and we would see what transpired in the morning. So we climbed into our bunks at 1:00 am, and I remember Stanley saying, "don't get too comfy; you will be up within thirty minutes to try something else.

You got used to instantly following asleep at sea, so it was a rude awakening for me when the buzzer, which usually woke us, sounded. I looked at the clock, and it was 1:20 am. I had been asleep for only twenty minutes. The chatter was, "George has launched a raft and is going to put a rope on the Mizpah".

We staggered up the hatch, bleary-eyed and to our amazement, there were two men in a liferaft just leaving the Sans Peur, paddling towards the Mizpah, pulling a rope behind them. They were halfway across when the Mizpah suddenly tipped over on her side, hung there for half a minute before upending with only the forward end of the boat showing, then finally slipping below the water at 01:25 am on Wednesday, 15th November 1978. I often wondered what would have happened had those men been five minutes earlier in going across to the Mizpah.

CHAPTER 5

Eyewitness Account from the Mizpah Deck

The following Is an eyewitness account directly from Jim Johnston, who was the chief mate on the Mizpah at the time.

This is a memory that I will never forget and will live with me forever.

Your description of the day is perfect and describes it as it happened.

We were trying to get to the lee of land as the wind was so strong and yes you are probably right in your description of that day that it was probably one of the worst days we had experienced at sea.

We, as you said, we were all in the wheelhouse together as the weather was nothing like we had ever seen before and even since retirement of my days at sea.

We were faced with a massive wave and it was like climbing the face of a cliff but on reaching the top it was looking down the other side of a cliff and when the boat hit the bottom of the cliff, so to speak, the boat felt as though we had hit a brick wall and it was a shudder that scared us all.

I went to check the engine room after this and could see water pouring through the Fish room bulkhead.

I immediately went back to wheelhouse and suggested to Rab to slow down so we could check out the fish room.

Dodging slow into the wind we discovered on opening the fish room hatches that the fish room was well full of water with boxes floating back and forth in the fish room.

I noticed on the deck beside the winch that deck planks had sprung and assumed that this is where the water was pouring into the fish room from the deck.

I imagined also that if deck planks had sprung that it was possible that some of the hull planks had also sprung open due to the force of the boat falling head first into a hole in the sea after falling over the wall or cliff of sea head first.

It was definitely the case that hull planks had sprung because there was not a chance that deck planks sprung would have taken so much water in such a short time.,

The picture still in my mind was we were looking down into a hole in the sea and it was like falling headfirst off a cliff face.

As you would imagine a freak wave would describe it.

As we look back now, we would consider ourselves very lucky to survive this ordeal.

What troubled me more than anything was the fact that Mikey Clark & Robert Junior were unable to get off her at first attempt from Jim Bowie of Millwood.

Because of the strength of wind, we were screaming at them both to jump when the boats came together.

Mikey had bad eyesight and his specs were covered in spray and he shouted I can't jump because I can't see.

We threw a rope to Mikey and shouted to tie this rope around his waist and to leave at least 3/4 fathoms behind him and tie the tail of the rope to Robert Jun because we could see he was in shock and he said he couldn't do it, he couldn't jump because he was in shock.

Next time Jim Bowie came against the Mizpah we could see that the top rails from the deck upwards had broken away and it was clear that the Mizpah was going down for sure.

We screamed at Mikey right we said when we say jump you must jump.

We had all the Millwood crew on the foredeck to help and when Mikey grabbed the rail, we found strength from somewhere to whip him on board the Millwood.

Because of the swell the two boats drifted apart and with a result the rope attached to Mikey came tight and pulled Robert junior into the water.

Unaware of this to skipper Jim Bowie he knew we needed another man and God knows where our strength came from, but we pulled that rope so fast that Robert was up at the Millwood rail in seconds and we just had Roberts legs in over when the boats came crashing together again.

Two seconds more and Roberts legs would have been crushed.

I am not a church going man Jim, but the good lord was definitely with us on that day.

It was not funny but looking back on the time to jump, when we all left the galley to go out into the freezing cold the last thing Mikey said to Skipper Rab was should I switch off the gas hobs on the cooker.

This was our only source of heat after we lost engine power.

By this time the water was level with the top of the main engine.

Someone once told me that if that had been a steel boat she would have gone down before water reaching that level.

That was a day never forgotten but we survived to tell.

My only disappointment of the whole ordeal was that Jim Bowie should have been given an award of courage and seamanship for saving our lives on that day.

CHAPTER 6

Bags of Dogs

We were all very quiet, as you tended to be on a Monday morning, at the beginning of a long summer day and probably a long summer week. Anticipating the next four days with perhaps only three hours of sleep a night was not a happy prospect. Then 'Big John' popped his head out of the wheelhouse and said, "John Slater is up and down with dogs". A strange statement, perhaps, to those who have never been at sea, so I had best explain.

Whitefish were light fish, and they floated when you towed the net up. Dogfish were quite something else. They are very heavy and sink. When you tow and snag something on the bottom, one of your ropes rides higher in the water than the other because it is stretched tighter. That is the first indication you have 'taken hold of a fastener.

When you are amongst dogs, you tow as usual, but as soon as you switch to high gear, the boat goes hurtling backwards until your ropes are straight up and down, hence the expression 'up and down with dogs'.

We never fished explicitly for dogfish, but most years, they appeared some week, just out of nowhere and then in a few days, they were gone again. They always seemed to be in immense shoals, and at times, you could have a massive haul of dogs one haul, shoot right alongside the next haul and not get a single dog. By now, you will, no doubt, have figured that to us, a dog meant a dogfish, not a four-legged furry man's best friend.

The year before, we had our biggest haul ever of dogs. The Dioscuri held four hundred boxes in the hold, which we filled before beginning to stack them on the deck everywhere we could. It took us around eight hours to get them all onboard, and the boat was very low in the water when we set sail for the harbour.

Once all your ropes are in, you may remember that I said you tow the net up. That takes much longer with dogs, and the net begins to sink fast as soon as you take the power off the boat. Getting the sweeps transferred to the power block is a considerable problem, and then the block struggles to cope with the weight. Frequently the skipper needs to tow it up again while you are hauling the net. The power block is simply an aid. It does not haul the net for you.

Once you get the sweeps in and get to the toe of the net, then it becomes easier. Long practice and learning led us to fit a 'dog rope' to the net. The dog rope was seldom used and was only for occasions like this. When you got it up, you connected it to another rope to the winch. The other end of the dog rope was connected directly to the cod-end lifting strop, allowing us to winch in and lift the first lift of dogs onboard. After it was emptied into the pond, the cod-end was retied and thrown back into the water, allowed to sink and fill with dogs again before repeating the process. This continued until you had all the dogs onboard.

When we got into the harbour, we had to start by boxing all the dogs on the deck to clear our feet. It was, once again, a long, laborious process, but finally, we were all done and landed a total of seven hundred boxes exactly, a colossal landing for us.

Back to the present, though, and John announced, "George is up and down too". This was George Runcie, skipper of the Ocean Challenge. That was one boat on either side, so we waited expectantly to see if we would have dogs. When we switched to high gear, sure enough, we went headlong astern, indicating a heavy load in the net.

John tried to tow the net up, but it was not rising very much. This load seemed much heavier than we had ever seen before. We tried all sorts of things to try and get the sweeps into the power block over the following hour, but nothing we tried worked. The weight was too great. So finally, John reluctantly came up with the plan to run the net out again with one coil of ropes, then attach the end to a Dhan. We would then return and retrieve the net in a few weeks when the dogs had either escaped or rotted.

Pause for a few seconds here, consider that we managed to haul a seven hundred box load last year, and consider how big this load must have been.

We ran off the coil of rope and dhanned the net, and then began fishing again with our spare net. The next haul, we had fifteen boxes of white fish (haddock, whiting, cod, etc.) and not a single dog in sight. Other boats around us were still getting dogs, though. Our third haul, once again, we were hurtling astern when switching to fast gear. Once again, the weight was so great that we could not get the sweeps into the block.

John was adamant that he would not Dhan another net, so he hatched another idea. We would tow the net slowly to shallow waters near the harbour, then when we stopped, the net would not have far to sink, and we would manage to get the sweeps into the block and haul up the dog rope.

There was one major problem with this plan. John was not at the front of the queue the day they were dishing out patience. Slow ahead was five hundred revs on the engine, and top speed was eleven hundred and fifty revs. John kept adding another fifty revs until we ran at one thousand revs.

When we got to the harbour, John briefed us, "get everything ready, and when I stop the boat, haul as fast as you can". When we hauled, it was effortless. Only the headrope of the next was left. The rest had broken away in the last sixty miles, probably quite near the beginning.

That, however, is not the end of the story. Remember the net that we Dhanned? We still had to retrieve that net. Three weeks later, John decided that the net had been there long enough, and we should go and try to haul it. We winched in the ropes, and they came quickly enough. There certainly was no significant weight there now.

However, before we got all the ropes up, the net started to come up with them, all twisted around the ropes. The net had been left for twenty-one days, and we later realised that there were forty-two twists in the gear, one for every tide change during this period.

It was a nightmare for us as we could not simply reel in the ropes. We had to place a strop around the whole lot and lift it twenty feet at a time. It took us hours, but finally, we got the cod end up, and there was only one lift there, not of dogs, but of many bones with rotten flesh attached. When we lifted it onboard, some men were violently sick due to the stench.

Our whole boat was stinking, we were all stinking, and when we pulled the net up onto the pier to try and untangle it, the overpowering stench permeated throughout the entire town. Once again, the Swackies were not popular.

CHAPTER 7

Broken Wheelhouse Windows

The Dioscuri had a strange look to her as the wheelhouse had been adapted to be high enough for John's six-foot three-inch frame. The shipyard cut off the usual wheelhouse and replaced it with a custom, higher fibreglass wheelhouse.

Instead of sharp definite corners, the corners of the wheelhouse were rounded, with the corner windows made of pliable Perspex instead of glass which would not be suitable for the curved opening.

By the time I joined the crew, these windows had seen eight years of successful service and had proved themselves a great idea, but that was about to change.

The prevailing wind in the UK is from the southwest, which means that sailing home from our fishing grounds to the northeast of Macduff was very often directly into the wind and heavy seas. In those days, boats did not have the complete protection they have now, being fully covered in and water/weatherproof. We had a whaleback and a deck shelter, but there was a gap in the middle which was open to the weather, and this area contained the hatch to the fish hold.

In poor weather, heavy seas would come aboard and flood the area and could also find their way down into the fish hold, having to be pumped out. If we were working, the skipper had to keep the engine speed down to try and minimize the amount of water coming onboard. He did not want to do this as he wanted to get ashore as soon as possible and get his fish landed.

I am not sure if big John would have worried about us getting soaked or having more difficulty working, but the threat of water penetration forced him to ease the throttle in a little until we finished working the fish.

On our last night, on the way ashore, we would be working the fish, and when we got to the last of them, I would go aft and get the dinner going. Usually, I would go aft, switch everything on, and then come back on deck. Once we got to the tidying up stage, I would go aft, take off my gear, check on everything, lay the table and many other things.

On a poor night, we would try to keep things simple, so no fancy pudding on this night; I would merely mix up some Angel Delight and open some cans of fruit to compliment the roast beef dinner. Dinner was well advanced, and I went down into the cabin to mix up the Angel Delight. As I started this, with it in a large bowl, whisking it by hand, I could hear the guys up above come in and start to take their gear off.

Some were in the galley, at deck level, but others were in the engine room, hanging their wet things up to dry by the engine's heat. I heard the skipper ask if everybody was off the deck, and then when he got an affirmative, he put the throttle full down. The boat had not even reached full speed when suddenly the entire vessel shuddered, hit by a massive wave, which engulfed the entire boat.

There was an almighty crash, and water started pouring everywhere. The corner window had broken, and water flooded into the wheelhouse with such force and quantity that it continued through into the galley and down the trap into the lower hull. At the same time, the partition between the wheelhouse and the engine room had many apertures for controls and instrumentation, so the water also flooded through them into the engine room.

I was in the cabin, mixing up the Angel Delight, which suddenly lifted out of the bowl and ended up all over the wall. I looked out the cabin door, which was latched open and was horrified to see the water cascade down the open hatch.

I watched as the engine room door opened, and Dodd Slater, who was covering for someone who was off, tried to escape the water coming into the engine room. He opened the engine room door to get out, but when he saw the quantity of water coming down the trap, he ran back in and closed the door again.

There was brief pandemonium, which probably only lasted for around five seconds before the skipper pulled the throttle back and turned the boat away from the weather. I think I was the only person on the boat who stayed dry, as the cabin was the only place that avoided the water. Even though they were soaked, the guys had to put back on their oilskins and go out and patch up the window.

The water had damaged our electrics with radios, radars, GPS, lights, and automatic pilot all ruined. Every electronic piece of equipment in the wheelhouse was utterly swamped and out of action. Being in the wheelhouse, Big John bore the brunt of it and was literally soaked through and through.

As skipper, we were never accustomed to seeing him change his clothes, and we found it quite amusing to see his underwear hung up to dry. I couldn't help but think his pants were so big we could have used them for a sail.

There was a significant delay before the lads finally sat down for their evening meal. It was all part of the job, though, and we just got on with it. When we got home, the skipper had to organise replacement equipment for all the water-ruined electronics before Sunday night.

Three weeks later, the very same window broke again, and we had the same process to go through all over again. When we got in that weekend, John had the opening plated and welded shut. It would never happen again.

CHAPTER 8

The Fishermen's Strike

Fishing had become problematic after the UK joined the Common Market, as the EU was known in the 1970s. Part of the agreement included the common fisheries policy, which has been hated by fishermen now for around fifty years. As a result, throughout the 1970s, fishing became increasingly tricky, and government regulation became increasingly tighter.

In 1975 there were huge blockades of all British ports, which resulted in some help from the Government, but did not address the real problem. However, the problems continued, and as the industry moved into the 1980s, unrest again reared its head, and the fishing vessels declared a blockade of Scottish ports.

On Wednesday, the 18th of February 1981, I had been sitting at home for three weeks without work and pay. The blockade did not seem to be doing any good, and the fishermen and the related shore support industry were the only people losing money. We were not affecting the Government, and they were not interested in a solution.

Early in the afternoon, the skipper called. "Be down at the boat for 9:00 pm, don't tell anyone and don't switch on any lights on the boat."

There were some pretty strong views on the blockade, and there was no telling what some men would do, especially if they had just come out of the pub with a good few drinks.

It would be much easier for us to go to sea if we could go undetected. It would, however, not be simple, as the Glendeveron was tied up with multiple ropes across the harbour entrance. The crews of the Dioscuri and the Be Ready would have to help move the Glendeveron out of the way to allow us to egress from the blockaded harbour.

We worked quickly, without showing any lights, carrying out all our routine tasks simply by the streetlights around the harbour. We concentrated on the essentials and left the unnecessary until we were clear of the harbour.

The Glendeveron had been tied up across the entrance with multiple ropes and many strong points on four piers. We had to untie the Glendeveron, escape the harbour, and tie it up again while drawing as little attention to ourselves as possible.

I don't remember any trouble, but there were reports of someone trying to stop us. I do not have any recollection of that.

We worked fast, cleared the harbour and on our way to the fishing grounds reasonably fast. For us, it was simply a typical week starting, but it would be anything but a typical week.

Nobody had been on these fishing grounds for almost four weeks, so the grounds were well-rested, and fish were abundant. We had never seen such good fishing, and we filled the boat in only four hauls and were underway for Macduff harbour Wednesday evening.

Around two hours (twenty miles) from the harbour, the shore lights start to come into view. At first, it was merely a source of light and undefined, but as we came closer to the shore, it became apparent that there were much more lights on show than we usually saw. Coming closer, we could see hundreds of cars lining the Station brae and vantage points all along the shoreline.

As we came within viewing distance of the shore, we could see thousands of people lining it, and we guessed they were not in a friendly mood. It was a beautiful night, and the sea was like a millpond. It was so calm we could moor the two boats alongside in the bay. Contact was established with nominated representatives on the shore, and discussions began about what we would do next.

It was agreed that a delegation would come out from the shore and negotiate a resolution to the situation. We needed to enter the harbour and land our catch, but the fishermen who had not worked for four weeks were angry that we had broken the strike.

The Macduff harbour pilot boat came out with four local skippers onboard who were tasked to negotiate a settlement. Unfortunately, my memory is a little fuzzy now, so I cannot recall which skippers came out. I remember Bill Watt and Maurice Slater were there, but I can't remember the other two.

We were all lining the aft rail as the pilot boat came alongside, and the representatives boarded. I recall Rab standing there with a twinkle in his eye. He looked at Bill Watt and said, "Well, Bill, you are aboard. Do you think you will get off again?"

Our two skippers and the four visitors sat around the mess deck table with a cup of tea and began to hammer out a deal. We needed to land our catch, but we needed their cooperation to do this safely. They knew that, ultimately, there was no way to stop us from landing our catch, so it was a case of a little compromise on both sides

Over the next hour, an agreement was made that we would be allowed to enter the harbour and land our catch, but our fish had to be sold by an independent fish salesman who would collect all the proceeds, which would then be sent to charity. That may sound very straightforward to you, but the practical outworking of that agreement was a little more complicated than anticipated.

As we motored slowly down the channel, the entire shoreline was lined with an angry mob who were baying for blood, our blood. Fortunately, the police had barriered off the entire long pier and the area around the fish market. Still, to get there, we had to negotiate the channel between the long pier and the Duff Street jetty, manned by angry mobs with as many stones and other missiles as they could carry, determined to carry out their revenge on us.

As we entered the harbour, Joe Watt began to go up onto the whaleback, where we usually put out a rope to spring us around the corner. Someone asked, "Where are you going, Joe?". "To throw a rope, Joe answered. "You can't go up there, Joe. They will kill you". Already the missiles were starting to rain down on top of us, and we had to take cover.

I don't pretend to know what was going through big John's head. He knew we were in danger, so perhaps he thought he would distract the crowd for a moment, but it was as big a shock for us when John released a distress flare right into the heart of the crowd. It landed behind the crowd at the foot of Duff street, and I think he was very fortunate that no one was hurt by his actions. However, it certainly distracted the crowd for a few seconds, which was all John needed to power the boat between the two piers and safely to the fish market.

The Be Ready followed us in, but the crowd had recovered a little and pelted them with assorted missiles. They had a rougher passage than we had, but we both eventually tied up alongside the fish market and began to land our catch. During the landing, the angry crowd continued to assault us with the only thing left to them, verbal abuse and insults.

It was a small town, and everyone knew everyone else, where they lived, what family they had, what type of car they drove and much more. I remember one angry protestor who was more vocal than all the rest, or perhaps just louder. Robbie Annan had been screaming abuse for two hours solid.

"Scanner", he howled, "you used to own a Mercedes, but it is a burnt-out shell now". Quick as a flash, John shouted back, "No problem, I have a new one on order". This type of abuse continued for the entire three hours it took us to land our catch and restock for the next week. Then we had to think about getting home. I can honestly say that it is the only time in my entire life I have been in the back of a black Mariah. Finally, the police obliged us with a run home.

Of course, the story doesn't end there. The fish had still to be sold, and the money sent to charity. Well, it didn't quite work out that way, either. It had been agreed that Alastair Paterson would sell the fish, and our guys went along with that. However, Jim carefully noted who bought what fish during the sale and tallied what each fish merchant had bought.

We were the leading supplier to most of these fish merchants, and it was reasonably simple for Jim to ring around them and tell them that they would get no more fish from us if they did not settle up directly to our office. Ultimately, we got paid, and no money was sent to any charity. The strike was broken, and most other skippers were too busy planning to return to sea to take much notice of this small item. And so the blockade of 1981 was ended by the Swackies.

The flare had landed near the Moray bar at the bottom of Duff street, and the woman who owned it, egged on by angry fishermen, pressed charges against big John. The case came to the Sherriff's court in May, and the Sherriff admonished John, which caused another minor uproar amongst local fishermen, and calls of corruption.

The entire episode was then consigned to history to such a degree that I could not find any reference to it, though I searched diligently online with many different search terms.

CHAPTER 9

Injuries

It has always been recognized that fishing is a dangerous job. I have already detailed tragedies where men have lost their lives, and entire communities are tipped into mourning. Yet, I have barely scratched the surface of all the heartache dished out to fishing communities around our coast.

Quite apart from the ultimate tragedies, there were also many day-to-day injuries and wounds suffered regularly. However, we accepted it merely as part of the job and got on with things as best as we could. I suffered a few injuries myself in my time, and although trivial, worth listing to give the reader an idea of what fishermen face daily to bring fish to your table.

On one occasion, I jumped down from the aft net box and must have landed wrongly. I went over the side of my foot, and pain immediately shot up my leg, which went from under me. I could put no weight on my foot and was convinced I had broken my ankle. There is not much you can do with it in the middle of the ocean, so I struggled as best as possible. Fortunately, there were no broken bones, and it healed gradually, although my ankle was weak for months afterwards.

We were well used to a rolling boat, and our bodies automatically moved with the deck, compensating for the vessel's movement. However, at times, a rogue wave would hit the boat with such force that the vessel would move unpredictably and cause us to reach out to brace ourselves.

On one such occasion, I found myself away from anything to grab onto and was hurtled towards the other crew who were gutting at the rail. Automatically, my arm and hand went to the rail to brace myself as I flew towards it, and I managed to hold myself against the ship rail.

Colin Chinchen had been gutting there, and as he grabbed support, his knife pointed upwards. When we recovered, he indicated his knife and said, "You were very lucky there". I pulled off my glove, showed him where the blood was dripping from my wrist, and replied, "perhaps not so lucky".

The blade had gone straight in, and although it was pretty deep, it was a straight clean cut which caused me no lasting problem. Forty years later, I can only notice the mark because I know where to look for it. I was, indeed, lucky.

I had a previous chapter on dogfish. They came with their own set of problems, not least of which was the vicious spike that they had behind their top fin. Often they came in such quantities that we merely threw them forward, then down the hold in large heaps. With so many dogs flying around, catching a spike was always a danger for which you had to watch out.

On one haul, a spike caught me on my upper thigh and tore a piece out of my leg. The spike itself didn't do much damage, but the wound got infected and bothered me for the best part of a year afterwards.

Once while hauling our net through the power block, a loose rope with a shackle fell from the block and hit me square on the mouth. It made a mess of my face, but the worst of it was internal. I just felt the teeth in my mouth disintegrate and felt like I had a mouth full of sand. Several visits to Albert Robertson, the local Dentist, resulted in several crowns to replace my broken teeth.

Knocks, bumps, scrapes, cuts and such were so common that most are not remembered. I was fortunate that these were the worst I suffered, or perhaps I was simply more alert to danger and quicker to avoid it.

However, it was more than just yourself. We were a steady crew, had been together for quite some time, knew each other and watched out for each other. That had a big part in the fact that I only ever witnessed one serious accident at sea.

Like all accidents, when everything is going well, then nothing happens. However, it adds to the risk when out of the everyday routine things happen. For example, the weather was always a present danger and risk we faced, and as mentioned before, we regularly went to sea in poor weather.

On one such day, a moderate force eight gale had given rise to strong seas and sizeable waves. We had seen much worse, and we had no particular concerns. Our ropes were all in, and we were towing the net up, and old Johnny Raffan complacently had one of his hands resting on the ropes. A particularly big wave went through, which caused Johnny to grip the rope for support. At the same time, the rope wraxed out through the steel roller and took Johnny's hand with it.

Johnny was in great pain and went into the galley while we hauled the net. It is the most dangerous time of the haul when you have a net near your propellor, so nobody could be spared to help him until the net was onboard. After the net was hauled, James, who had done some first aid, went to Johnny's aid, examined the damage and helped him bandage his hand up.

Johnny had two fingers amputated, and the rest of his hand was in a mess. So we hove to for a while. James worked with Johnny, and John radioed details to others around us. After a while, John looked out and asked Johnny, "Are you OK?" Fishermen are not ones to admit weakness and always play down any pain or injuries, so through gritted teeth; Johnny replied, "Y.y.yes, I,i,i'm OK".

With a cheerful voice, John replied, "that's good. We will just continue to work away then". James was very unhappy with his father as he knew how bad the injury was. It was almost two days later before Johnny had his wounds attended to in a hospital. After that, he never returned to the fishing again.

As previously mentioned, we were fortunate to have had little to no injuries onboard. Unfortunately, most other boats did not fare so well, and chapters could be written detailing the many injuries suffered in the industry. However, this is not the subject of this book, so we will leave others to tell of these things. Conclusion

CHAPTER 10

Summary

Those stories are from the late 1970s and the early 1980s, forty years ago. What has happened since then to the guys mentioned? Sadly I am the only remaining member of the crew of the Dioscuri from those days. I was the youngest, but still, too many of them were taken before their time.

The first to go was big John, then Joe Watt. James suffered a heart attack and died at only fifty-two years old. Although the oldest in the crew, Johnny was a tough old horse and outlasted three of them. Colin Chinchen died five years ago, and Stanley Ross followed only two years ago.

When Stanley died, this spurred me to tell these stories. I figured they would be lost forever once I was gone, just as that way of life is now. However, fishing is an entirely different ball game now. It is no longer a cottage industry but a complex, high-cost industry where only a few fishing families have survived.

The Swackies in Whitehills continue to have a fishing boat, with two of Mitchell's grandsons skippering the vessel on alternate weeks. But, of course, there is also much to take care of ashore these days, and

John Louie and his wife Mary are still involved in helping out ashore, whether it is getting in the stores, picking up and dropping off crew, or a thousand other requirements.

In Macduff, most of the family have moved on, with most of them involved in the oil industry, either offshore or onshore support. The entire area has changed. In the 1970s, the fishing industry employed thousands of men along the coast. Now only a handful of men in this area are engaged in fishing, with the oil industry becoming the principal employer.

However, the sea is in our blood, and many of the men, once involved in the fishing, have taken up careers in the marine industry, either on rigs, supply vessels, standby vessels or many of the marine support services required by the oil industry.

A few have even embraced the sea as a hobby or pastime, with many owning small creel boats, which the local harbours now rely on to fill their berths. Personally, I had had enough of fish but still loved the sea. So I opted to buy a small sailing vessel and have already published a book on my adventures under sail. I will include a bonus chapter of my book, "Sail with Jim", at the end of the book.

Before you read the bonus chapter, may I ask you a small favour? If you have enjoyed this book, can you go to Amazon and leave a review so that other people may find and enjoy the book?

https://www.amazon.co.uk/dp/B0BTRPGRGG

CHAPTER 11

Bonus Chapter - Sail with Jim

If you enjoyed this book, you would love the sequel, actually, the first book I wrote. So here is a taster for you.

I am not sure how old I was. Certainly, it was a very long time ago from my now 61 years old. It must have been around 50 years ago, probably around 1970 or thereabouts.

Early on a fine summer's Saturday morning, Albert Robertson, a close family friend, and also the highly esteemed and very well-respected local dentist arrived to pick up my cousin Robert and myself to go sailing on his small yacht which he kept in Gamrie harbour. We were going to sail the yacht from Gamrie up to Banff.

Gamrie is the local name for a village in the north-east of Scotland which has the real name of Gardenstown. The village was founded by the local superior, Alexander Garden of Troup in 1720, and is today regarded as one of the major influences in the UK fishing industry.

Albert owned a holiday cottage in the neighbouring, but smaller village of Crovie, and berthed his yacht in Gamrie harbour during the summer. I don't know which model of yacht the "Kittiwake" was, but I do remember it very clearly and estimate it at around 17 feet long. It had a drop keel and an outboard engine if I remember correctly, but things are starting to get a little fuzzy now. I suspect it was a Leisure 17 or similar type of yacht.

It was all white with a small porthole window forward in the cabin at either side. Whoever had painted on the name, you didn't get computer generated vinyl graphics in those days, had made a very good job of it, and on each side, up forward on the hull, not only was the name prominent, but it was proceeded with a very good picture of a kittiwake.

It was like going on holiday. I was so excited. I had been around boats all my life, my dad and my entire mother's family being fishermen, but this was different. This was a yacht.

Maybe these ocean going sailors would laugh at me, but if a boat had sails, to me it was, and still is, a yacht, regardless of size, and yachts were exciting in a way which fishing boats were not. There was something about going through the sea without any engine noise, peaceful and quiet, free and gliding like a bird soaring on the thermals.

This first trip kindled an interest in me which was never to be suppressed, and although it was to be another 40 years before I bought my first yacht, the deal was sealed on that day.

I am not sure how long Albert had owned the yacht, but he certainly seemed to know what he was doing and imparted some of that knowledge to our young heads, as best as he could. Albert would sit at the helm and instruct Robert and myself in handling the sails and ropes.

The "Kittiwake" was a light responsive boat which sailed well even in light winds. Around our coastline, there were thousands of Kittiwakes, a small seabird, like a miniature seagull, but cute and without the harsh predator look of the bigger bird. Albert pointed these out to us and explained where the yacht's name came from. There were literally thousands of birds which nested on the cliffs of nearby Troup head, which has since been declared a bird sanctuary.

I am sure we had some sandwiches and drinks packed somewhere in a little bag, as we were always hungry at that age, but to tell you the truth. My memories don't extend to trivial little items like that, but to the more important things.

We travelled down to Gamrie in Albert's Citroen. In those days there weren't many foreign cars on the road, not like today, so the car was a bit of a mystery too. I don't think I had experienced much beyond Ford, British Leyland and Roots cars. For young people who don't remember, Roots was the name which Chrysler had at that point. I won't even try to explain British Leyland; you will have to Google it. It really is a different world 50 years down the road.

Arriving in Gamrie, 6-7 miles from our home in Macduff, we wound down the brae in a small village which was completely different from our home a few miles away. In fact it was so different; it could have been in a foreign country. The culture was different, life's pace was a little slower, and they even seemed to speak a different language.

Albert seemed to understand the language though, and know the locals, so perhaps we would survive. Little did I know that only about 10 years later, I would marry a young girl from this "foreign" village, and less than 20 years later, would move to stay here with my family.

Driving down the steep brae, you could see the harbour long before you reached it. It kept disappearing and re-appearing as we wound our way round the ever descending hairpin bends on "Gamrie Brae". If you are reading this book, and have never been to Gamrie, then I have to say, you have missed out on one of the most beautiful spots in Scotland.

Make a plan to visit, but best do it in the summer, as it can be a very remote and bleak place in the winter, like many of Scotland's treasures.

We eventually parked up on the pier at Gamrie, and the harbour was full of little fishing boats. Most of them were small creel boats (Lobster pot boats for the English), but right there, out in the middle of the harbour was the Kittiwake. In fact, many of the boats were out in the middle of the harbour. I wondered how the owners got to them, and how we would get out to the Kittiwake.

We stood on the pier and looked out to the Kittiwake and I hoped that I didn't have to swim out to it. We did swim a lot in sea in those days, and didn't mind the cold, but I didn't have a towel with me today to dry myself, and I had no "dookers" (Swimming trunks).

Albert took off to the south pier and we toddled behind. He located a rope on the pier which he loosed out quite a bit. Back to the East pier where another rope was located and pulled in, bringing the Kittiwake right alongside a ladder so we could board her.

I was in my element. For the first time in my life, I was on-board a yacht. Young though I was, I would begin to learn a little about how a sailing boat worked, what all the ropes were for, but right now it was all a mystery.

I am sure Albert must have had some preparation to do before we were ready. There was a small red tank with fuel we had taken down with us in the car, and down the ladder. I guess that had to go somewhere. To be honest, I don't remember a whole lot. I just remember untying the Kittiwake and leaving the ropes attached to a buoy and the ladder to be retrieved later when we returned with the boat.

Actually, we never returned to the buoy. Although we did make this westward journey a number of times, we always left the boat in Banff, so I guess someone else must have sailed the boat back with him, or maybe he did it single handed, like I tend to do on most of my trips.

With the outboard engine running, we motored out of Gamrie harbour into the shelter of the "Muckle rock", which guarded the harbour entrance. We rounded the rock, and once out into "Gamrie Bay"; we got the sails up and shut off the engine. We began to move along by sail power only. I don't have a date, a time, or even a year, but this was the exact time when my love of yachts was born.

We sailed out of Gamrie Bay and out past Mhor head, one of the two mighty pillars which dominate and guard Gamrie Bay. In Gamrie bay, there is a strip, just a few miles wide, which is made up of crumbling red sandstone. This strip runs about twenty miles inland past Turriff, and you can tell where it is, as you can see the old houses made out of the red stone. At Gamrie bay, at the western side, you have Mhor Head, a craggy outcrop which separates Gamrie from Greensides, a long sweeping rocky beach. On the eastern side, you have the massive granite headland of Troup Head, which is one of the most important colonies of sea birds in the north of Scotland.

High up on Mhor there is an ancient church, "The Church of St John the Evangelist", which was built to commemorate a victory over the Vikings at the point of Mhor in the year 1004AD. The "Battle of the Bloody Pits" was a resounding victory against a foe that were pretty formidable, and the skulls of three of the Danish chieftains could be seen in an alcove in the church walls until about 1970, when the skulls were stolen. They were subsequently recovered but are now kept in Banff museum for safe keeping.

It is amazing how different places look from the sea, as opposed from the land. If you are planning a visit to Gamrie, then do try to get a trip out to sea to view the village from there. One of the local creel boats will oblige, and you could even have the opportunity to help them pull their creels. I remember my days as a fisherman and when you looked along the coastline at night, from the sea, Gamrie looked bigger than some places ten times its size, simply because it was built on a hill.

The house I have in Gamrie now is at the top of the village. It is only about ¼ mile from the harbour, but it is up at 140m, or around 450 feet in "old money". From the sea, you get an absolute spectacular view of Gamrie, the entire village. None of it is hidden. Each part is higher up than the street below, so you see it all. At night, from the sea, it looks like a city, even though there are only around 200 homes there.

I am sure Albert had sailed this route a number of times before, as he was able to keep us fairly close into land and keep the trip interesting for us. Round Mhor head, heading west, you come into "Greensides", which is a long sweeping bay, full of rocks with no possible landing place for anything other than a very knowledgeable local with a small boat. In days long ago, there was some salmon fishery carried out here and there are the remains of a salmon bothy at the far western side of the cove. There is also a very rough, steep track where some poor horse would have had to pull up a cart loaded with fish and equipment, and even their boats. The cliffs which surround Greensides are all around five hundred feet high, and any time I have been down there, I was always breathing very hard before I got back up to the top. For this very reason, it is very much an unspoilt beach.

There are a series of bays like this all along the coast, each one different and interesting, and all the way to Macduff, including one which opens up into a series of gorges containing all the water which makes its way down to the sea from the area behind all these majestic cliffs. These are known as the "burns of Cullen" locally. The furthest east we had ventured as kids was the "Salmon Howe", but our mothers didn't know that. That was the sort of place you hadn't been told so, but you just knew, you weren't allowed to go there. It was a desolate deserted cove where, if anything were to happen to you, then you could lie there a long time before you would be discovered. It was east beyond Tarlair, up over the golf course and down the other side.

We sailed past the "Salmon Howe" and into the bay at Tarlair. Now we really were into home territory. We spent most of our free time in the summer at Tarlair outdoor swimming pool, one of the finest in the country, in those days. I remember summer days with Tarlair absolutely packed with thousands of people, pipe bands playing, galas, paddle boats..........those were the days. We would spend all our free time in the summer there, and even after school went back, we would rush home from school at four o clock and be changed, a quick bite to eat and off across the golf course and climbing down the cliffs to Tarlair in as short a time as possible.

The cold never seemed to bother us much in these days, and I begin to wonder about the kids today, and even about ourselves. Is it the introduction of central heating which has made us softer? I don't really know, but right through until the pool closed at the end of September, we would be there until they shut the gates at 8:30pm every night. Our mothers never had to wonder where we were in those days.

Just off the big pool at Tarlair, there is rock, right in the middle of the small protective bay. Albert expertly took us right into the bay, inside the rock, even to 20- 30 feet from the poolside. All the Saturday bathers look at us. Nobody had ever seen a boat come in there before. Robert and I had to stand in the bow and watch out for any rocks or boulders and shout back to Albert at the helm, so that he could take evasive action.

So we negotiated our way around the rock and back out to sea, in full view of envious bathers, some of which were our friends. I was on top of the world, so proud. Every one of those young boys eyes were glued to us as we sailed in so close to them, and then sailed off again. It must have been high tide, as I have seen that whole area dry with very dangerous looking rocks many of other times.

From there we continued our way past Berryden quarry, the "Black cove" and The Black Cove was another of these places you weren't allowed to go. These were the days before environmental awareness, and this was where the town dust cart deposited its load when it was full, straight into the sea.

It really makes you wonder. We have cleaned up our act so much these past forty years, and all of a sudden there are no fish in the sea, which had thrived there for thousands of years. Could it be that we are not as smart as we think we are, and we are actually interfering with nature and changing the order of things which have gone on for centuries?

Between the Black cove and the back of the harbour at Macduff there was a rocky beach, all of which we knew intimately, having scrambled over the rocks many times, fallen in, tumbled and gained many scratches, bruises, bumps and cuts, none of which I remember or did me any harm. Well, there was the one time we got cut off by the tide. I managed to jump across and only got my legs wet, but Robert hesitated a little too long, and in the end had to strip off, throw across his clothes and swim. He was just getting dressed again when our mothers appeared on the scene searching for us. It was well past our bed time, dark and they were pretty agitated. Hey, it was all good fun, part of life's learning curve, and in the end, we are still alive, aren't we? Mothers worry too much. So do wives!!!

Continuing our sail, we had to sail out past the "Collie rocks", which are a pretty dangerous set of rocks just off Macduff, mostly submerged just out of sight unless it is a real low tide, then out across Banff bay before taking down our sails and motoring into Banff harbour and tying the Kittiwake up. Fifty years later, I still remember this day, the day which introduced me to my expensive hobby. Albert, if you are reading this, my wife says you have a lot to answer for.

www.ingramcontent.com/pod-product-compliance
Lightning Source LLC
Chambersburg PA
CBHW072103110526
44590CB00018B/3301